Composition
in White

for I.R. Bell

'There was almost no departure from the text book either but the cover driving, the cutting, the pulling, the lofted hits, the back foot push, the delicate nudge to third man were a form of cricketing ecstasy.'

Stephen Brenkley, *The Independent*, on Ian Bell, England and Warwickshire batsman.

Contents

Let the torn poems sail from you like a flock
of white egrets in a long sigh of relief.'

Derek Walcott, *White Egrets*

'Does there not also exist a poetry of ecstasy, even a
poetry of lunchtime cricket as a form of ecstasy?'

J.M. Coetzee, *Youth*

I
Springtime of the Nations

Springtime of the Nations

A sympathiser advises a friend

The lilacs were in flower, heavy, drowsy,
boulevards suddenly pleasant. And
I suspect the sun was out. You must
understand there was nothing we could
do. In the square hung the conspirators,
dangling effigies – the partying over –
how they caroused our masters,
the hubbub was like the explosions
of military battle to deafened soldiers,
we the defeated drank deeply while
the victors were clinking glasses. All
we could hear was the *chink, chink,*
like raindrops in gutters, of their toasts,
and vowed never to let glass touch glass
again in Hungary. And so my friend –
I remove my drink from your pleasure
in my health – in due homage
to the twelve – the silence between us
heavy, ominous. In my hearing, glasses
will never chime. All through the night
they were pushing the boat out, the oars
of a thousand hurrahs dipped into water,
chink, chink, chink, chink, chink,
came the replies of the tiny waves.
It was terrible music to the demented.
The boulevards next day were ashen
with pollen. The twelve hung in the sun.
You must understand there was nothing
we could do but shun the moment,
to turn our backs on all that merriment.

Looking Glass Street

The rooms were lofty & across the street our songs drifted
as if by coincidence into the realm of Number 6.

We weren't short of breath in 1916 safe in Zurich,
we were soldiers of the absurd – Dadaists, refuseniks –

chanting timeless choruses of '*etc ad infinitum*'
slowly and solemnly in the cathedral of our cabaret.

Across the street at No 6 close by, the Bolsheviks
deepened their plans & Lenin at his desk was at work,

accompanied by our siren songs, the purposeless
fundamental world of laughter, beauty and atoms.

We burnt our boats in a bonfire of the vanities, no rules
allowed. Our ridiculous hats, our quixotic gestures,

lived on the same street, on the Spiegelgasse.
We opened a gallery & Lenin moved under cover

in his closed train to St Petersburg, the revolution
bursting the banks of the Neva; he was never so free,

nothing was accomplished and nothing marred,
our songs were in his back pocket like bombs.

Long Island Iced Tea

for Yvonne Leathley

Like ex-pats on a sundown terrace
we drink Long Island Tea,

the colour of shingle;
in its cloudy depths

lurk the piranhas of vodka, gin, rum and tequila
and let us not forget triple sec;

once in the blood they slay
the unwitting partakers of Tea;

in the cocktail hours it will lay
you down until 5 in the morning,

a night passage without remission;
it will leave no trace, no recall,

an eternal blankness;
this is the allure of Long Island Tea,

the colour of river water
where spirits contend with lime and coca-cola,

wrestle in the cloudy chamber,
the glass glistening with icy power.

Like ex-pats on a sundown terrace
we drink Long Island Tea

like a suicide pact
like a doomed class observing ritual.

Barbados

At the Windward Club

They're sitting under trees,
black figures in the shade,
watching cricket.

In Barbados everyone knows
the minutiae of the game,
its cathedral interior;

the form
of England County players,

and they are watching Bell.

Boys are collecting empties
by the boundary.
It's a tidy Club and they're proud.

A guy keeps passing
and stops to argue and shout.
They're affronted by Stanford

who came to their islands
to steal their money

and their cricket.

He's not the only one!
The anger is rippling from Antigua.
His private playing field,

his Xanadu, his patronage,
lord of all he surveyed,
using the head of a black child

to support his autograph.

What flickers to mind
are the shadows and ghosts,

starving under trees,
as Belgian masters
accrue ivory,

in Conrad's *Heart of Darkness*.

The cognoscenti nod their heads.
No need to run. No need to run.

Bell takes three boundaries
like chopping down trees.

Judgement of Paris

Through the windows of a dream you were sitting
among three. An inconsequential third was next to you,
but your rival was this assertive finger pointer.
He was standing like someone who has always haunted me,
taking charge, his authority an easy coat to slip on
and it hung on him tailor-made.
In human shape you were in the middle,
your eyes still trembling from dependency. Nothing
to lift your countenance, without the magus inside.
I was carefully folding the fabric of life
as it rattled off the loom, folding and pressing each scene
into a picture gallery wrapped in cloth. He
was standing like a righteous angel blessed
with tongues and a message, and surely won
the apple of my approval until his lips closed.
Your eyes were hovering at the edges of my attention,
the past safely bound up like a parcel in my hands,
and of the past there was something to tell,
and of the three there was only one to choose.

A picture in my mind of the Windward Club,
on the lee of the island, in Barbados,
a place sacred to its undertaking
without a border of concrete seating.
The cricket field edged by trees and some
canopies. It was the apple of my eye.
Black faces in leaf shadows,
or under awnings. The warm wind
blew eddies of applause.
England were playing without ceremony.
I was struggling with my vision
of the loveliness of the outfield at the Windward Club,
as you were listening in human shape among three,
words sinking into your comprehension like soft rain.
A field lightly bounded but still deserving status.
Capacious, I offered like a present.
Your face acquiescent.

The Slow Master of Lenin

He cut my hair into shapes of a Japanese fan.
I am unrecognisable to myself.
He said I am the slow master of Lenin.
He is a fast bowler who never smiles.
We are barricading ourselves within moving walls.
It was not a dance. It was life or death.
We had to move quickly. We were strangers
introducing ourselves. I was lissom with dark hair
onto my shoulders. He was a revolutionary stylist.
We talked theory as we ran from room to room.
He cut my hair as if I were a mannequin.
As if I were someone to shape. I looked haunted
by scissors. What have you done I asked him.
It was done. The mask I was given I could not remove.
We had met in a dream tantalisingly a step ahead
of those without. There were pursuits of a kind.
I am French for princess. French for teacher.
French for woman. French for betrayal.
Who was he? This chrysalis of my imagination?
Who am I? I am shorn and bereft.
He said I am the slow master of Lenin,
why not the fast I quipped.
He showed how fast. It was an act of love swift
and to his taste. My hair cut into blades like grass
awry in the wind, like treason.

Letter

Where was the glamour?
The hotel had stained carpets and German food
for breakfast. We searched for café au lait and croissants.
I remember Paris in the 60s and the wonderful aroma on the streets.
I still can't believe outdoor tables and waiters weren't waiting for us.
We hunted down *La Maison de la Poésie*, a purpose built bunker.
Even the white house with Picassos was full of quickly moving on
tourists. We were at one

with the modern drift of consumers.
We could have turned all this into poetry but failed to write
even a letter.
I remember you stomping back up a street in your shorts.
Some moment of temper
propels you. Where could you go with your head full of Apollinaire
and no Left Bank or Bohemia to abide in?
We ruthlessly went to churches.
In Montmartre there was a woman singing and banks of candles.

There were spats about the exchange rate not in our favour.
Only in a recommended restaurant did we find Paris.
You marvelled over pigs' trotters. I ate pale slices of duck
with clusters of tiny onions. I could hardly imagine the devotion
of peeling them with patience. Even the pudding
could not compare with the delicate transparent beads

I had crossed a channel for.
We are in the Communist quarter, you declare,
and turn a corner to a street market full of bundles of herbs.
Harissa has to be bought and the word on your tongue
is fiery and Moroccan. A bottle of *Cassis*
to lace the champagne you no longer drink. But it's more

a chance to remember those touches of glamour
to replace the fizz.
You are down to recipes as you stroll the stalls.
I wish I could pick them all up and take them home for you,
the pursuit of these gourmet touches
in a poor backstreet for anyone and everyone.

Seeing Everything So Damned Warwickshire Clearly

Late in the day even though it's spring and light at eight,
my Warwickshire eyes, one definitely not as sharp,
read well enough the whole complicated mess and clear
as a bell your distress and contamination of doubt.

You're talking so directly I wince while experts extract
misgivings of syntax but *Dead Man's Handle* is the safety
brake. My Warwickshire eyes, born in Brum, bred
in Leamington, were relied upon to read the belated truth:

love isn't the passenger but driver of the headlong
out of control last train to Demonville, that was the deal
signed in blood at midnight. No brake allowed. And once
on board we had no business hoping for stops at stations.

You were not to blame, despite forensic evidence.
I saw everything so damned Warwickshire clearly
we knew one day I would sit and read the poem at dusk
to understand conclusively that all was written by both

of us, not in the stars nor in the sand but on stone
with a chisel, like the mason in *Briggflatts* who found pens
too light. What's buried will die misunderstood
by readers of runes. The poem decrees we were of a kind

to surrender again at the drop of a hat, too tit for tat,
too independent, too passionate, two half souls, one coin,
two romantics and two realists. But you were cold eyed
with foreknowledge. When I jumped off the train you smiled.

II
A Word for Warwickshire

for John and Jill Pearce

A Word for Warwickshire

She gives me five words to take to Warwickshire.
But none fit. There is no magnificence in tiny fields
hedged with many trees, stable, enduring, no
provocation from the village cricket pitch closed
down for winter, or even a little shambles in the
orderly fireworks and roped off bonfire. Only flames
have ancient tongues, ceaseless, primeval, talk
to the air but nothing quizzical. They die down,
brooding over ashes like wolves over their kill.
Is there a paltriness in my contentment to be home?
I breathe the air of Warwickshire at the end
of a lifetime, passion no longer my concern.
In dull November, the trees expose their bones.
I take my age to my birthplace. The traveller
looks back towards home, writes Po Chu-i
in his little poem. There is a word, *Topophilia*
coined by geographer Yi-Fu Tuan from *topos*
(place) and *philo (love)*, a love not insignificant.
My mother tongue comforts me with its chime.
I brood over cadences of my lost parlance –
there is no word for Warwickshire except time.

Grand Union

for Jen

Drifting at slow pace to Birmingham,
the canal dwelt at the bottom of the field,
we called it *The Cut*, our local waterway,

nearer than the river. Swimming baths
were toxic with warnings of outbreak
of polio. We eyed the languid brown skin

which had oozed round the Gas Works
into these outskirts of pastures, flowers
and hedgerows. A dip was our name

for breaking that skin and we lined up
in knickers. All day we jumped off
the low bridge, oblivious to hours,

out of eyesight and earshot, the hot
summer day never waning to warn us.
I would pay for our pleasure, wrath

of my father waiting at home, but then
he was always angry at something
or other, so the rebel was born.

The Grand Union led me astray
into a lifetime of ignoring orders.
Our entitlement was handed down.
    Kids play until the cows come home.

Stars and Stripes

They wore those beige cotton uniforms, the Yanks.
Ironed trousers, neat hats aslant, they were turned out
compared to our heavy worsted lads, they were clean cut,

smart and didn't tramp. We brave kids, desperate
for a treat, asked for gum. They never declined, slid
from a pack a slender silver-lined wafer, pristine as
their shirts. We curled the free strip upon our tongues.

What did we look like in our wartime togs, a gaggle
of Brits, brazen and curious? Our garments not washed
or ironed until Sunday. Scruffy, smelling of earth,

half decent in socks and sandals. We'd learnt
what to say, the magic formula: *Got any gum, chum?*
Our faces not aware of begging, there was a war on.

We were a ring of compatriots, somehow we knew
our rights, children were exempt from decorum.

War Damage

In memory of J.W. Litherland, coal merchant

The blackout was his. The lack of moonlight,
the lack of stars his. He never spoke of the mine,
the war came along with a tide as black as coal,
with a shore of slag and sulphurous craters.

There was no talk of hundredweight sacks
on his back, the cloudy grime, the grim life.
His ailing wife in the Home for Incurables.
Strength hung on his big frame. Grandfather

under Birmingham skies, night conversation
of *thud thud* and *crack crack*. What was *sorrow*
when men were dying at sea and in the air?
Or *hardship* down in the back streets of Brum,

the city of a thousand tall chimneys like a fleet
in harbour, the city of a thousand slums
in a cloud of its own making? The war made
his life ordinary, gave freely and to everyone

his childhood spent in the mine, the 11-year-old
not entering school but below Griff pit
with his father, breathing fear and thick air,
hunched like the children all over Britain

in buried tin sheds at the bottom of a garden
the war had sprinkled like fairy fungus, and hung
around our necks the daily reminder that gas
is just around the corner of our lives as it was

to him, not the *gas, boys, gas* but the sudden
dousing in the dark or the last bright flash
down tunnels overarched with girders
like bony ribs, or the curved tin roofs of shelters.

Moonlight Sonata

In memory of the medieval city of Coventry, destroyed 1940

The lamp of the full moon enters the sky,
the opening movement of invading night,
the rising moon at the appointed time

searches Coventry under the moonlight.
The three spires' high needles, the parks
all quiet, the shopping streets with blinds

down, the cobbles silent, the workshops
and back alleys all dark, at the centre
the spike of the cathedral like an arrow

in its heart, the Bayley and the tucked in
skirts of its ancient lanes, the black
and white timbered cottages and fine

houses like shadows of history leaning
together, all banded inside the line
of the old city walls, tied with the knot

of an invisible girdle, the encirclement
like the outer circle of a target. How

like a gunshot the wailing sirens alter

the calm. Starlings sprung from the eaves
fill the air with patterns of alarm. Coventry,
its face woken to the lamp of the moon,

still complete, travelling to the universe
like a ray. A drone interferes. Across the sky
wingtip to wingtip an iron mantle. A drone

eight miles away to a child not asleep
in a shelter. The city still whole, still breathing,
like an innocent face, a still turning page,

all history in place as the avenger drones
the *Moonlight Sonata* twinned in tone
to the prelude of Guernica in the afternoon.

Over the cathedral the sign of the crosshair
as bombers usurp the sky, the birds,
under their wing a new city of fire, the core

tied in ribbons of flames like a gift
to the people of Coventry, everything familiar
already a ghost rising in smoke, the loss

of a thousand years left to the light
of the morning, the moon calling on the night
to remember, the moon of Goya

and Picasso, warning of the ambush,
the reprisal, the lamp extinguished
like a lament, a broken promise, a sonata.

Eight miles from the city, the All Clear
brought out families from their shelter,
into the not yet dawn of November,

the siren calling like an alarm clock to
the unsleeping. Awaiting them a baptism,
like a blessing, for half the sky had turned

scarlet and before her father lifted her up
onto his shoulder, before a word, before
they saw spearheads of the flames,

she tasted in the closet of her chest
the breath of their foreboding.
You'll never forget this, her father wishes.

Like something she was born to or born for.
The cathedral was blown apart to the walls
as if its heart failed by the morning

for old and new living together like strata.
On its own debris and dust the city gags.
The island of the centre had vanished

as if the day was confused and delayed
to put back yesterday. The city of Godiva
parading ruins like a beggar in rags

asking why am I so punished.
The day did nothing but rain on dead Coventry,

like a lament, a requiem, a kaddish.

Coventree

Coventree is forever a nocturne –
dying overnight under hammer keys

of black and white, no searchlight
stronger than moonlight, all cities

are levelled into dust and built again
says the poet in old age

but the broken music of Coventree
is unplayable. What's gone is gone

and how the nocturne droned *on*

and on and every stone and brick
and every beam and fragment

of lath and plaster, every mullioned
window and ancient stained glass,

every porch and courtyard, every lane
under curfew of the wailing siren,

flew into the air as if to heaven
and into a history of atoms,

flew into the immaterial world
of music – into a nocturne forever,

the lament of the *Moonlight Sonata.*

The lineage of Coventree
has not even reputation, no homage.

The city of a thousand years
awoke into a diadem of ashes and smoke

reversing time into dust
every speck, every particle of the city,

blown like a dandelion clock losing
its crown, clouds of time floating away

into the corona of the *Moonlight Sonata.*

May Morning

In memory of Hazel Litherland

The dress was white lace
like falling snow when air
is quite still. It was wrapped

and boxed during the war.

Black-out nights I
would walk out onto snow
with my daughter under

a blizzard of stars. Flurries

on my wedding day
fogged our pictures,
no recollection

of the bride in her dress.

Sometimes I would open
the box, empty of everything
except hope, all the ills

had flown into the world.

In the spring, the first
after long years of war,
a spring of bridal hedgerows

opening star garlands,

we had no finery
except the flowers. For
my daughter, chosen

to attend the May Queen

I took out my wedding
dress from snowy tissue
layers and cut it down

without sentiment.

Clockwise

for Marilyn Longstaff

The impossibility of going home,
back to the war zone and Brummie aunts,
under Nanna's hegemony and chiming clock

which authorised our hours, plangent
yet strident, it insists the day comes in
quarters. All I have left of Christmases

cooked in the small kitchen by the bevy
of sisters, somehow all of us in the second
floor flat with bare boards in the attic.

We arrayed ourselves in the lounge,
a family that likes to drink tea and chat
under the eye of the clock. None of that

keep the best for Sundays, the lounge was
for everyday wear, the suite crammed in,
with laughter and smoke from cigarettes.

The clock was a vital cog in the wound-up
world of bombing, its grand walnut dial
was not to be out-whined, standing firm

for Brummagem values targeted by Nazis.
Every Christmas the siren would call us
to run down the stairs, run round the front,

through the entry to the long back garden.
There half buried the shelter awaits but
it is pitch black and the long queue of aunts

is impatient. My mother's foot is searching
for the step of the upturned box which has
vanished. We can hear the stick of bombs.

Hazel! They all push and gash my mother's leg
against the corrugated metal. The bomb lands
in the graveyard over the back lane, killing only

the dead because we're all inside and find
the box on my Aunt Esme's foot. She wants
everyone to *hush* so she can hear the bombs.

We know it was close and next morning inspect
the great cavity and the moments that exist
between life and death; a few yards and timing.

A Birmingham Symphony

My Nanna sits at her piano. Her arms are as broad as a cricketer's,
one who heaves sixes over the boundary, her lips are clenched
and downturned as though in disapproval. But she's concentrating.
Her girls are at her back, Stella and Esme, singing harmony.
And even my mother might be there and Auntie Bel.

They're crooning *Blue Moon*. Nanna is thumping out the tune,
her curls are like crotchets, in iron grey rows. Her hands
are firm and decisive. By morning she is marshalling steel pans
in the works canteen and bantering with directors of the board: *I told
him*. Freedom flows from every gesture, she's cap in hand to no-one.

Background

Halfway up the hill on Railway Street, wagons shunting
by the back gate; 2 up 2 down, the usual high narrow
stairs straight onto the front door, the tiny parlour
and huge fire, the scullery bestrode by the giant iron
mangle with a wheel to rival a bicycle, *Great Granpa*
and *Great Nanna* sat in ancient order, unmoving bookends
to the tableau of the range which brimmed with coals
and knockback heat. A railwayman's house under the eye
of the station where the Expresses blustered past,
each one checked with the watch on a chain decking
Grampy's rotund paunch, 'On time' or 'Late', a tic
of his former life on platforms. I played with the mangle
or out the back across the tracks, epics of let's pretend
between vacant trucks stranded up sidings. The sunken
back yard and outdoor lav, carefully strung up squares
of newspaper on the door. Neatness pervaded the grime
of the soot flaked air, combusted from a thousand high
stacks and low and the trains with their comet tails
of fire, steam and grit. The parlour's high temperature
suited us when warmth equalled welcome. Always
there was tea. The chenille tablecloth glowed like sunshine.
Nothing seemed to alter. Nanna's hair gathered in a net,
she always wore a pinny, she had the kindest cushioned face.
Grampy opposite. His heavy white moustache tinged
with yellow. He puffed on a pipe as he spoke and listened,
happy with smoke as the stuff of his livelihood, smoke
Brummies coughed on and added to with furnaces
of their own and cigarettes offered like cartons of cachous,
each chalk stem pure in the snug, trailing descant plumes
and blue haloes languidly drifting over our heads, smoke
which struggled to escape and outside terraces gleamed jet.
    A miracle then, the patch of lily-of-the-valley by
the front door, they thrived, the thick clumps of pendants
and scent, they liked their spot, a step or two from the privet
where Great Granpa might stop by his gate, the orchestra
of trains his music, Birmingham a symphony of factories,
and at his feet the white bells of the old Forest of Arden.

The Pink Dress in the Window

Amid the ordinary days after the war,
walking home from school without the fear
of sirens, the long walk passing a small shop
of bric-a-brac and second hand clothes, in
the days of early autumn, I stopped to look,
in my let-down school uniform, the hems
like tree rings, in my bleached blazer.

There was a pink net dress in the centre
of the window, pink as candy floss,
with a pink satin sash and maybe a bow.
It was the star of the window, calling
to belong like an orphan. I ran home, afraid.
I was suddenly consumed after years
of indifference bred in shelters and

lino-cold rooms, everyone in the same
boat, I was madly in love with pink tulle.
A new hunger, a post war confection
of impossible dreams, yet reachable
in the cast-off to tell to my mother. Next
day it had gone, leaving a hole in the universe.
I stared at the emptiness, my shock.

Two weeks of walking to school and back,
two weeks of solitude without the frock,
two weeks of not growing used to love's
yearning, the shop on the street was vacant.
At home my uncle made a special cake
with lattice icing. He was a Co-op baker
and he wrote my name without shaking.

Who was I? A girl who had left childhood
behind in the war, my frozen childhood,
we were all waiting for the war to be over.
On my bed a cardboard box to be opened
like the future. The pink dress unveiled.
Wonder at the simple miracle, the price
was paid, and the price will never be paid.

Romance on a Sunday Afternoon

My days are measured in plates from the dishwasher.

The January sun is over the roofs. I will walk in the Vale.
My muscles are waning like skies at dusk. I retread paths.

And vow to my body promises I will never keep.

My spirit flies like Bell's lofted cover drive over the heads
of fielders. There's no sense in happiness.

I'm glad I lived between two worlds and with many
passages. The feckless joy of my Brummie aunts who worked

in shops and offices and canteens. My mysterious Nanna,
she who presided over her piano with fingers like sausages
she cooked daily for workers. She thumped out tunes.

The chorus was her daughters, Hazel, Beryl, Esme,
Stella and Janet. Two were songbirds. Their laughter
a waterfall over rocks, cascading and splashing,

changing necessity into fun. In the attic was a box.
I was drawn upstairs to the room of empty boards
and a trunk. A discovery of treasure. The sun is gone

meanwhile, the clouds gather like smoke at one,
the hour declines and I haven't eaten breakfast.

In the box, heavy lidded with studs, were costumes
from an unknown theatrical past. (Why did I never ask?)

Would the ballet slippers fit? A wartime child
can never decide between Columbine and the Soldier.

I shake out her gown of rose-budded thistledown,
parade in military scarlet and gold braid uniform,

clack in red tap shoes. My mother chose the heavy blue
satin number with ruched cuffs, my auntie Beryl always
the butterfly. There was a harlequin. The trunk was bottomless.

We sang party pieces at gatherings like a wandering band
of itinerant players, a commedia dell'arte with Brummie

accents. I never questioned the romance and the gift
I keep alive. In my wardrobe are clothes for dressing up.

My other world was sitting at desks for scholarship.
A lifetime of doors to open and some I could only knock
on. What keeps me here inside is too long at my desk

with poetry and cricket scores. The sun sits low on terrace
roofs and the Vale will be cold. Some stoic impulse insists
I leave the poem and the room, as I respond to marching

orders and slate skies, the brittle branches will knit today
a fairisle of light and shadow. I tread the pilgrim's way.

My aunts would sit in cars for Sunday afternoons, just long
enough to do the rounds, then back to put the kettle on.
The fire still glows. The toast would char against the bars.

Shepherd's Hey

I can whistle, I can sing. I can do most anything.
I can dance. I can play. I can do the Shepherd's Hey.

Can you do most anything? Lanes weave
the slashed pasture together and hedges
knit up the small parcels of fields; trees
are left to brood in the meadows, farmers

avoid their fairy curse. Frost and wind
have not dislodged the leaves tunnelling
over roads. Gold, red and rust painted
on the glass of air, the sun shining brokenly.

Can you do the Shepherd's Hey? Streams
leave ribbons in the grass where we knelt,
our little boats stampeding to the pond,
where they sank or circled the water

unsure where to land. The woods and
glades, hedgerows and spinneys are
tatters of the Forest of Arden, kept
by tradition uncleared. Custom

hides the roots. At edges of railway
and road Warwickshire holds the line,
the footfall treads old paths, old tithes,
into the deep past. Shakespeare wrote

Warwickshire into verse, its banks
of flowers fit for the bed of Titania.
All we have left of that pastoral
now the flowers are gone, are losses.

Bundles of bluebells bleeding from
the back of my bicycle, childish
ceremonies of May Queen and consort
in fields crowned with hawthorn,

hidden copses and dells of violets with
a secret door, the golden honey of cowslips,
the pale complexion of primroses, the fragile
mauve of lady's smock. We chewed

vinegar leaves and stalks, and sucked tips
of clover. Warwickshire bred us,
her tunes rarely listened to but familiar
in the blood, in the tongue, the rustic

rough music, the dances we never danced
and sang, *Shepherd's Hey*, in Morris troupes,
the old dances, and the old music our
forebears knew, distant fiddle and drum,

and lilt of tapping feet, is recognition
which halts me in the street when a busker
calls on pipe and tabor and I'm in tears
for home, far away from my fallen England.

III
Forever Young

Forever Young

for Derek Walcott and Ian Bell

Sea manes toss in sympathy with his decadence
in old age, but his lack of prudence and his infatuations
comb the beaches for a clean page to write his guilt. The sea
will wash it every day. I applaud his groans and his romantic

fires ever seeking a new muse and half wishing like Yeats
to be redeemed from the last desires. He pursues, or not,
the young and lissom and hides his lust in despair, while I
greet the start of the season and watch young men play

cricket standing like narcissi in the grass/ without regret
I love beauty from a distance, at the boundary edge.
And today my muse marries his bride, his bat put aside
that delivers an electric shock, brilliant and precise,

scorning the need to run, his wrists twist in rhythm
to hold the flourish. The pleasure in his graceful *pas
de deux* at the crease, for he is wed to cricket and
dances at his own wedding. Today he takes another bride.

My sea is calm and untropical. I salute the great master
whose egrets arrive like fresh hopes, and still arrive,
his heart still an apprentice and innocent. I am wise.
I have written in the sand my signed resignation.

'Caprice on the Arizona Border'

rendezvous with a line from Elizabeth Smart's
By Grand Central Station I Sat Down and Wept

If moonlight is strong enough, cricket played under moonlight
is surely a pastoral caprice; strangers, or bandits, hiding in whites,

under their arms a roll of carpet, mark out the circle of their secret
game, carrying bundles of sticks, two bats, and the famous ruby

ball. Between them a chain of 22 yards laid as sanction across
the Arizona border staking their claim. The teams like ghosts shake

hands. The carpet is unrolled like a prayer mat to the moon. No
sound but the mallet knocking. The stumps aligned and the bails

reverently lowered into their niche. Like Bedouin the players wait
under canopies, the desert waits. Someone has drawn in the sand.

The game is silent, just the footfalls as the bowler runs, the tap
tapping of the nocturnal bat and that chord as leather strikes willow.

The desert moon will reflect on the ritual, the deep desire to summon
a field, to measure the pasture, to anoint the gates, while shadows

flicker in the guise of exiles performing this instructive dance,
like insects or birds repeating their song, this ceremony of home.

Night Vision

They leave behind imprints, the 22 yards of outline, the run up,

the marks of the slips, lonely fielders, and the wrestling floor
of the wicket keeper, the rim of the boundary as full as the moon.

And what of batsmen and their high steps to the centre? In parallel
are the dragging creases of their return, their time in the centre over,

for this is a stage where men might preen and a moonflower opens
with bats like stamens. We read the structure like a fossil but cricket

is capricious, prey to the deviation of an air current and fragile
as a moth's wings to collapse at a touch. Uncertainty is at the heart,

uncertainty in the flight, in the grip, in the back lift, in the sheen
of the ball, in the earth. They set the game up like gods and let it live.

Composition in White

for Ian Bell

At Cardiff where the wind and bowler are leeward
and billowing rain has cleared the blue stands,

at your feet is marked the wound of a deep groove
and in your scrutiny you look outward and inward,

do not question the importance of your next move,
this stationary moment only partly in your hands.

Few are watching as the ball answers your passion,
seeking to break past all your rehearsal: the arrival

of the Belovéd, for without the game's intercession
you could not dance like an angel on an atom

or even graciously kneel against that repeated
hurling and twisting cast at your feet, a mystery

only read in a near moment of greeting; on the stalk
of that intransigence you emerge like a flower.

This is by way of introduction a meeting of minds
and to acknowledge I am reading your stroke play

like verse and without translation, the interest and
disinterest in your eyes tells us you are composed.

And I think of how particles are entwined at great
distance and move in synchrony and how the poem

is serene, all the letters queuing up to be known.
At Cardiff you wait in transition for all outcomes,

to open a new page, each time a fresh beginning
on this field where three principles compete:

function, uncertainty, beauty, and the rain
has drawn back its final curtain for your innings.

Clap Bellhead Angel Boyhood

a line from *The Book of Demons*

All the non-fans nonplussed because they had already written
their little parodies, their impersonation of demon tongues,
plenty of them out there, in the ether of the internet where
misery lurks vying with discontent for room on the page,
the waggish jokes sure of applause from other like minds,
tripping over themselves to be first to scorn the batsman
who can never do enough to please. But the words died.
Randomly the book opens: Clap Bellhead Angel Boyhood.
He disappoints all the demons queuing up to score their point,
their little stings, their winks so sure 0-1 is not the time
to come in and 14-4 will swallow him up in the backwash,
in the tidal reach that is Edgbaston when it finally stops
raining. The tide too strong from the arms of Durham
bowlers, racing to end the day. And 15 wickets falling like
so much flotsam. The laughter was ready in the wings,
the tittering in anticipation, the failure written
in the gloom, the bad luck of being out there. Ho, ho,
here comes the chorus of dwarfish lad bumpkins,
linking arms, crowing behind their pseudonyms
until Bell got his 50, and in the darkest of hours next
afternoon between downpours like curtains closing on
a tragedy, in the just not raining light that worried umpires,
Bell struck two fours to end his drought, and before the rain
decided enough was enough and fell incessantly,
the scoreboard signalled 106 not out, to be resumed.

The Bride

Dressed in white, forever poised, the heart
of my cricket is a bride. Are these her suitors
courting her inclination? When they stroll out
or when I glimpse the whites on green in some park,
the romance aches to be told in courtly gestures.
Here are her swordsmen and here her artillery
and foot soldiers who have discarded weapons
to enter her chamber; they take up the masque

and the strains of the game; cricket has this heart

they play for. I forever sit at the window
of my admiration, advised that coming upon
the stationary moments of cricket,
when we are waiting with the players
for the commencement of the action, the bowler
before his run, and we have the patience
to consider the position of the fielders like captains,
and cricket is set out on the grass
as a long process where time is a dowry

for the bride, the initiation of love
is not momentum, but courtesy.

The XII Days of Christmas

for Gillian Allnutt

On the first day of Christmas my true love sent to me
A willow from a rare tree.
On the second day of Christmas my true love sent to me
Two slender bails
And a willow from a rare tree.
On the third day of Christmas my true love sent to me
Three stout sticks
Two slender bails
And a willow from a rare tree.
On the fourth day of Christmas my true love sent to me
Four cover drives
Three stout sticks
Two slender bails
And a willow from a rare tree.
On the fifth day of Christmas my true love sent to me
Five stolen runs *etc.*
On the sixth day of Christmas my true love sent to me
Six slips a-leaping *etc.*
On the seventh day of Christmas my true love sent to me
Seven sixes soaring *etc.*
On the eighth day of Christmas my true love sent to me
Eight fielders fluffing *etc.*
On the ninth day of Christmas my true love sent to me
Nine bouncers bumping *etc.*
On the tenth day of Christmas my true love sent to me
Ten wickets falling *etc.*
On the eleventh day of Christmas my true love sent to me
Eleven men a-weeping *etc.*

On the twelfth day of Christmas my true love sent to me
Twelve scribes a-scribbling
Eleven men a-weeping
Ten wickets falling
Nine bouncers bumping
Eight fielders fluffing
Seven sixes soaring
Six slips a-leaping
Five stolen runs
Four cover drives
Three stout sticks
Two slender bails
And a willow from a rare tree.

Winter Trees

for Ben

The yard acquired the leaves,
fallen like snow, inches deep.
They were clutter and needed clearing.
More were to come with the breeze.

She worked for hours, packing her purposeful bags,
thinking of nothing, thinking of cricket in Sri Lanka.
Sweat dripping from the hair of Ian Bell
at the base of his helmet.

So intimate.
She took the leaves to the dump, ferrying autumn,
the day not particularly cold;
the familiar road, and the turning;

and didn't lift her head from hurling leaves
into the skip,
without pain or enjoyment, or anything
close to feeling, until she saw the winter trees.

The winter trees in their plain beauty.

They stood watching like a Greek chorus
surrounding the workings
and the waste gathered in,
their summer reduced to silken mush.

But I thought nothing of this. I just stared
at the winter trees and they stepped
into my mind forever and were everywhere,

on the outskirts, on the roundabout,
and by the supermarket. At home
it was time for highlights of the cricket.

2007

IV
Winter Trees

Geraniums

I heard the winter birds flutter in the almost black trees. Still

there was a smudge of rouge in the sky to south and west,
refusing to fade. I am rarely on the balcony in the twilight,
in the low ebb of the year, night pressing on me, closing
down this little space to a cold hollow. No thoughts. Waiting
for the last light as if crimson would bleed away quickly; and
I was a prisoner of the lingering sunset, the sun gone long ago.

In the end I left the sky as it was, stepped down into the pit
of the dark yard where sparse red flowers were breathing
by the warmth of the window, their dry leaves pungent and
familiar but I could not name the plant, my mind suddenly
opaque but could describe their holding on beyond
the curtain of frost, sun-loving flowers, not autumnal

chrysanthemums nor michaelmas daisies, they leaned
awkwardly, top heavy, nameless, as the bush or tree stirred
with hidden birds. I was waiting in deep dusk for the light
to come on. The scarlet velvet petals gave me no clue,
nor the rangy stalks and bruised aroma of old vegetation.
In Spain they live long. I put them under my bed once for winter

and uncovered a shelter of white threads probing for light,
blind things, so now they take their chances outside the window,
no longer forsaken in their absence, the nameless ones.
The cold is taken inside on my cheeks and hands. Later I climb
the steps and the sky is black, light completely gone, no
lessening, the moments when the embers died I missed.

Durham in February

Snow was still around; in tatters;
a walk to the river to the dark bank;
the water very deep brown, bovine.

The trees drew up from the opposite
curve of woodland like taut sentries
in brown and white uniform;

along the river raced a skiff, a snow white skiff,

the rower dressed in white dipped
his white oars in the calm chocolate water,
the oars flashed like underwings of birds;

the river held the cameo: the air river-fresh,
snow edges at my feet, the frieze of tree stalks,
the monotint of winter

yet underpainted surely
with the not yet seen spring;
the oarsman sped lightly, a phantom briefly,

a skiff, a snow white skiff, like a sleigh.

Collecting Stones

A glade of snow, the cream sky down over the hills,
we were entering winter like a secret door into the past.

Reassuring cameos of blue, this was a blizzard
that would not last. The grandsons wrapped up like

Eskimos were talking to hens sheltering under a bush.
I was afraid of the roads, the car stuck in the tight lane,

the snow was settling its small grains, like Easter money
to the poor. The boys were intent on reaching the quarry,

intent on the stones the water had beached: a cornucopia

of granite, sandstone, carbon, quartz, shale, limestone,
Frosterley marble; they were cognoscenti, collectors,

weighing down pockets. Stones thrown into the water,
exploding bubbles like deep bombs, they were deep

in thought, the boys, they had a purpose in that ring
of hills that bled away, at their feet the constant notes

of the beck bubbling like a dawn chorus absorbed into
their stone myopia. We threw snowballs, gathering

crusts of snow from left-over drifts as the sun ruled
one line of stars on the water, a break in the weather;

lungs of clear cold air, sky patchy, life taking a breather.
Snow is a time traveller. This was the way we once lived,

journeys up the Dale, sky nets of snow, and distant pillars
of light: the stones we turn over, pick up and take home.

Dark History

Long forsaken upland this moor of spoil heaps
and fog, high in the Pennine chain, once the haunt
of lead miners. The fog's wraiths hang dankly, rain

clings in wisps like the forgotten breaths of puffed
out lungs. This fell the lunar landscape of *Killhope*,
the all weather mine where boys worked outside

in the washing yards and their fathers fell ill
with trench foot or TB, wading through tunnels
in clogs, the dispiriting turn of the century

before warfare added killing fields to wretchedness;
they must have yearned to escape to France
and found themselves in the same desperate mess,

with no way out but over the top to the bayonet
and machine gun nest. The fog swirls on the road
like gas, a dark presence broods here, a high up

lonely distress that still seeps through the air
and down through rocks to drip, drip, into hollowed
out caverns in the hills. They weren't paid enough

to live and wives farmed a patch to feed them,
all the calamity hidden. It's a place of suffering,
it's in the old machinery and bunkhouse, the cold

streams and isolation at the top of the world,
where they must have felt abandoned by the alchemy
of progress, the workings of enlightenment lit no

candles here, just enough to see ledges and seams.
The spoils and hushes that curdle the fell tell us
they just moved on, leaving pit scars to weep.

It was never reclaimed like fields of Flanders.
Dreariness left undisturbed by the flanks
of this road, so that Kill-hope, the old double name

of Celtic and Saxon for high pass and upper spate,
seems once more a fretful warning to long dead
drifters squatting on Alston Moor not to enter the gate.

A Stone for Bill Martin

'No Kingdom without common feasting'

A pebble speaks in tongues on a poet's
coffin, a stone to add in line like beads
on an abacus or last words of an epitaph

or a random haiku written in stones.

Pick one. A stone can translate
into a flower. Stones that rattled in sea wash

for one who walked the beach and sang.
His poems stride out with Caedmon
taken step by step, each stone a throstle.

What is custom, this stone, this flower?
As if we know a ceremony as simple
as a daisy chain or necklace around a throat?

Gesture nurtured in the hand, a stone
to chuck or cast or sit in admonishment
on a table, or laid in a row instead of sorrow,

a path of pebbles in blind testimony.
Feel the weight Bill, each one a drop
in the ocean, each one an unbuckled clasp

from the spine, and will survive the fire.

A Page Still Turning

A thin old man with a white summer cap stands erect,
his face austere like Saint Cuthbert on the Farnes;
out of a box, beautifully tooled, he cradles a concertina
with straps of flowered ribbons he hangs round his neck;
his poise is serious. He plays the Morris dance, the lilt
as crisp as steps we can't see, there are no dancers
to accompany him. A Morris Man, embroidered
flowers and ribbons tell us he's no ordinary player.
The music stops. He is very old, his face unbending,
his eyes like birds on a rock, like one who keeps faith.
Like one who decorated the gospels on Lindisfarne.

Choruses from the Last Bus Home

for Ann Coltart (après Eliot)

At the violet hour or is that violent I may digress,
at the eleventh hour in the city, I saw so many undone,
the clocks all silent, the thin clad ones, sans overcoats,
seeking shelter in timeless queues to the entrance halls
of domed palaces or is that doomed where one or two
were given the nod by ageing pugilists and so consumed
beyond my vision. So many undone by the happy hour
who now tread unwarily through ancient streets where I
see prawn cocktails overthrown amid the clatter of heels
downward to the river, all the unquiet at this hour with
eyes like shining pearls dredged from the deep, all
scuttle unsteadily like sideways crabs on cobbles,
forgetful of the pavement's edge, lurch to the river
in the busman's path as we pause to consider and
nearly connect with the painted finger ends of typists
freed from their desks and their undergarments. O
I have seen it all so many times. Gerrump, the bus
growls a low note of thunder, the sans-overcoats press
unheeded, and some unheeled, in endless throng
as we approach the midnight hour not yet chiming
from watchful towers above Tyne waters. Shall we cross
to the other side? I do not think so. Chug Chug.
The unsleeping tread on the wishes of others *ad infinitum*
turgidly like sluggish tides in the empty docks, flotsam and jetsam
in no hurry. A game of chess is not on the cards but I see
in the violent hour that no one bids goodnight to ladies
or closes the premises with Time Gentleman Please.

V
Red Thread

Red Thread

Her shawl was too rough,

rough around the neck
like a thistle or a nettle;

yet beautiful as first light
through branches or a screen,

a screen like a prayer window,
grey-brown chequered with white,

an off-white like snow on the second day;

the shawl woven from mountain sheep
rough as hands too long in water,

pliant worn hands that bristle,
the shawl coarse on the throat,

easy on the eye, cast off and picked up
like a child, a difficult disobedient child;

the shawl with the temperament of a goat,

the fringes like a goat's beard, but a hand
had stitched there a single red thread,

the colour of blood, as if a pact was made,
a finger pricked to sign a seal,

something rendered, a devotion.

'The Unbroken Surface of Snow'

An imaginary film set to music by Andrew Cronshaw

A young woman, more woman than girl,
beside her nomad tent, is ready for her
journey. She is childless. Tradition

demands she must walk beyond shelter
onto frozen wasteland. The Frost-slayer
will impregnate her or let her die.

She is unaware she is being ritually
discarded by her husband. Snow
is falling in splinters. She has to offer

three gifts: a lock of her hair, a silver coin,
and anything unwanted by the barren. Her
husband has watched her disappear

from the settlement, a vanished speck
still living in his mind. His wife buries
her ringlet in the sparse snow, tosses

the silver coin as libation and unravels
the undyed wool of bootees which
streams around her in disorder. She must

prostrate herself. The snow is no more
than a brittle coverlet. Anonymous
the wilderness, the crevasse in the tiny

ravine where she lies down disoriented
and snow blind. Next day her husband comes
to collect her body. The air is as clear

as glass. He finds the unravelled wool
disordered like the broken surface of
snow. She is still alive. He lies on top of her

to give warmth until he is drained. He ties
their bodies together on the sleigh
and orders the horses home. The sleigh

is an ever moving line, lightly drawn
in the landscape, until snow discovers
the tracks and cancels her appointment.

The Box of Spells

In memory of Julia Darling, died 13 April 2005

for Annie Wright

The box slips from my weakened fingers
into a vortex of jumble, two sharp pencils fall,
a tiny doll clutching a scroll I prise open.

Tell your worries to this doll it says. I refold
the note under her stiff little arms. A bundle
of coloured sticks tied with gossamer pink

thread, a paper plane made from a map of
Mid-Sussex, 2 dried rosebuds, a pearl button,
sea-frosted glass and a flat pebble. A stamp

claims *I know my body better than you do.*
A green label warns *FIRST AID KIT
FOR THE MIND.* A buff card addressed

to me: Box Launch, The Biscuit Factory.
Unopened since 2005. I read at random.
Don't walk in a straight line. How to Deal

with Terrible News. Tell the doctor a joke.
I have to carefully repack your poems
in pink tissue. I spot a silvery green ribbon.

Nothing quite goes back the same way. My
fingers are impatient, clumsy, quavering.
This lucky box will undo harm you tell me.

I find the recipe for A Curative Soup 'well
seasoned with tears and a secret'. The tissue
paper has somehow become old and split,

aged and careworn in the box, invaded by time
no charm can keep distant. In the Isle of Wight
you have a memorial bench. We borrowed you.

The luck was ours, the North a stopping place.
The box of curiosities spells out your gift
I bought for a friend, untouched by prescience,

who now lies in need of all its medicine. Who
knows, Julia, if one scrap will tip the balance, one
pearl button, one tiny marble, rolled like dice.

Box Hill

for Catherine Fuller

The day was generous. Warm, sunny, a gilded upland.
Our university days lay like a wreath on the grass.

Four women climbing out of working lives,
out of motherhood, sisterhood. The years climbed with us

although we didn't notice, the past already heavy,
the future foreshortened, the future we now live in,

your tired haunted eyes not looking backward,
as you stride patiently to the shops and cinema,

like a habit, as if living must be a habit, a custom.
We talk of *Emma* and you plan your funeral

like a picnic for friends, like the outing to Box Hill.
I hope we lived in the present with our books

and learning, four women who were light-hearted
who never returned for their reunion.

I think of it raining, a light autumn rain that lasts
all day until everything is soaked to the leaves.

We slide the bed onto the balcony into the sun,
surely September's blue sky will ease her?
Her rigid legs sheltered in brown slacks,

her right hand twisted inward like a strange sea
anemone. Her thin crying, like a wisp of smoke
from a packed down bonfire, belongs here

in the hospice garden, in the purple bushes
of the michaelmas daises that will be dead
before she is. *Take me in*, words are few,

the unhurried purgatory we cannot
hasten, says the doctor, as her cries scent
the hospice with faint autumnal smoke.

She's sleeping, exit ordained, nurses move like wraiths,
link her world to a transparent tendril on her wrist,

lift the heavy blanket of suffering, hers and mine,
as the motorised bed shifts like punctuation

in her dying, still tenderly raising and lowering her legs
as if she were capable of complaining. *Intolerable*

the nurse said. *Intolerable* when all she could convey
at last were cries, the first signal a mother hears.

I tell her she's entering the British Library, walking
towards me, tall, elegant, self-contained. Our lunch
will be something healthy. Or we are in Chelsea

visiting the Physic Garden behind high walls, stroll
between the orderly beds, with names surviving centuries,
offering the cultivation of sanctuary like her final room.

Lines on 'Already Broken'

She was 'already broken', the Buddhist text
advises. Her rooms in Clapham North
revamped exquisitely like the perfect

cup and saucer in a tea-set. But the street
was dingy and on its doorstep drugs
might overflow at night. Her back yard

a coil of light and honeysuckle. Just so
her books, her frosted glass, her slim figure,
kept life out and something precise within,

something of an educated class,
a little of Hampstead, the Left-wing kind
not quite vanished. She was 'already broken',

a dangerous flirtation with a theatrical past.
Her life had not conquered sorrow. Not regret
just a crack of bitterness in her façade.

Her poise made every visit pleasure,
the white carpets, and white chairs, ornate
fireplace, and dragonfly lights on the mantel.

The German Hotel

On the iron-grey sea a single black sail, *vela,*
an unlit candle; like the dying wish of Odysseus
who could not rest from travel. He lost
his fireside companions: they all said *No*
and put their feet up. He's on his own,
crossing a strip of bone-white sunlight
like a splinter silhouette of the lone sail
in a pirouette of a ballerina, arm and leg raised,
in contemplation après-spin.
Even in the dark sea, the sand bleaches through
like the skin of the woman we saw mottled
from burns, patches of tan and bone-white.
The rocks gnaw at the sea edge, grinding spittle.
The hotel is keeping us tidy. Straw parasols in rows,
the guests are mindful to park their towels, guard
their spaces, walk everywhere not in haste.
The bright pool has been captured from the sea,
tamed like a house cat. Today we can hear growls
of the ocean, the waves prowl, extend
white claws. We stay in the harbour
of ourselves, the hotel with blinds, German TV
in all the rooms, and our faces like locked doors.
Clouds are drawn to the sun like prudent parents,
screen violence on skin, hover tenderly with soft
grey towels edged by bone-white needlework.
The sky is scratched by chalk. I swim nerveless
in hotel waters. A skeletal boat on the horizon
is like a death ship or my future foreshortened.
Would Odysseus pay the bill for his shipmates,
shipwreck plans for drinks in the bar, and take
his old age out to sea, strike the sail, alone,
and by sparks of stars find his way home?
Home not being the hearth or hotel,
but the wilderness beyond; not imitating death,
plenty of time for that, an eternity.

Notes Towards a Death Bed

for Antónia Melis Cursach

On her pink pillow a fresh flower is placed each day.

Her skin illuminated within as if by a candle, the skin
not papery, but silken. Her eyelids are finest gossamer.

She is breathing an occasional deep sigh
as if her lungs were apologising for her late arrival
in the deep caves of her coma.

Her mouth cannot speak, gapes,
her old age at the frontier,

at that strange crossing. Her face
has lengthened into a painting by El Greco,
as if the moon is dragged by water, blooms with death,
like white satin petals of the church lily.

She must be at the shore of the mythical crossing. Her unseeing eyes
do not open. The boatman has yet to come.
The smell of the river greets her.

One by one the vital organs are closing down
as if little shops have no more customers,
no more chat at the counter, no more Antonia

calling behind her shutters, *Sí.*
And her never changing dining room to enter
like a still life painted 50 years ago,

the candelabra, the oil lamps, the heavy framed paintings,
the rocking chairs, the cool tiles.
We sit contentedly as she moves in her house, a tall slim figure
straight backed like the chairs, she is bringing *cava*
always called *champán* and the large cake-size *ensaimada*.
The children eye up their portions.

Above her breathing we talk of Antonia and my mother,
two ladies dressed to kill as they restaurant on the *Borne*
and an eyebrow moves when we mention she was pretty.

Laughter covers her like pristine sheets
and is fragrant as the new flower on her pillow.
Laughter is the last thing she will hear from us.

Adiós Antonia, who walked as swiftly as a soldier.
She is walking into the woods behind Es Carregador,
my mother and she, disappearing into the pines,
their dogs joining them one by one, Sam and Frankie,
and Beauty rescued from the sea and bound together paws.

She is gone, not to the crossing, nor is she at the river,
that is not her country. She would not leave Capdepera,
its scents, and the square where her father drank coffee,
the narrow streets, the shuttered houses, perched
on the hill under the sentinel castle.

Unchanging Capdepera, unchanging Es Carregador,
receive Antonia into your streets and woods, into the cafés,
especially the Oriente and the old one with *leche fría.*
Receive her for drinks at the Aguait, for *paella* at the Tennis Club,
for *lechona* at La Torre. Receive her for *calamares* at the Marítimo,
and receive her onto the terrace of La Esquina

where the sun rises into her eyes,
where the full moon will always appear
like a fresh rose on the pillow of her sea.

VI
Edgeland

Edgeland

The waves are wading to shore, they've heard the news,

the flaying of the flute player, the waves are shedding
the crime in choruses of foam, seas are wrathful
and streaming with tears, milk churned to cream stringing

and lacing the waters, the weeping of sap of the woodland,

rivers tell the seas across the wide edgeland of coast,
the crossing of tales, metamorphosis of transgression,
the flaying of the flute player; tears of the nymphs

reach the shore. We stand and stare, humans in bondage,

the sea's life its own, beauty carelessly composed in
wreckage of itself, the waves are a white cloudy symphony;
his music played and replayed, the sea is untiring, each trill

captured on the scissor sharp swell and flayed to crescendo.

We could bathe there, in the flowing asses' milk, in the icy
nerves of the North Sea, in the broken awakening of Marsyas,
bellowing. The sea could cripple us, skin us alive

Whitby

We compare the sand to khaki, the sea a middish brown,
a camouflage of khaki and white, the air drowsy with drizzle,

and misty foam blurs the wave tips, Whistler could walk
his dog here. No entertainment but the snow of the waves

and bridal veils dragged over the shoreline from wives
disappearing under the breakers. It's quiet and calm

but the sea is seething an argument with itself, waves
rushing far out and smashing hot headed into white lava.

It's a muddy riot of dull colours, lathered in cream.
There is so much white for Whistler. And khaki.

The view deep in blousy waves, endlessly unbuttoning.

Black Kesh

We're all standing in line at the Black Kesh, 2 am stars blink
in the darkness. Drinks all hurriedly collected to the back,
cries of !The Garda! !The Garda! It needs double exclamation
marks in this foreign tongued land, the police with guns motion
us to the front of the long whitewashed barn somehow
hollow in the night, suddenly abandoned, we're all outside.
It couldn't be more remote – in the dip of fields where lakes
glimmer and paths cross to the pub under moonlight and stars.
The Garda know hours are unconfined here, in Monaghan
close to the border, you would think they had something to fear.
A tip off, but we're thin on terrorists. Locals and artists and poets
dance to old fashioned music, old waltzes. The furniture's
those brown leatherette seats which never softened
and kept their hard silhouettes through years of swing bands.
New rounds of Guinness just ordered. Whiskeys in hand,
the chat in halos around the tables. The talk of the Irish
was hurling. A plain place. We had left rooms in the stately house
like absconders, preferring the dark route to a lounge and lazy fire,
the well trodden path over fields to lights of the Black Kesh,
the road to experience and here we were lined up, naming names
and far away addresses as the Garda considered us and the fact
we were outside in the night air with nothing in our hands.
They searched the empty bar and the empties. Dismissed us.
Drove off in their big vans. New drinks were poured, glasses
clinked and time to marvel how quickly everything had been
despatched, all evidence washed up, how practised
the locals were at hiding the obvious. All we had to do was obey.
All stains smoothly wiped away like contraband, or guns.

1994

Legends

'There is a legend here that the Woewater only flows in times of war and dire trouble '
Richard Mabey, *A Brush with Nature*

In memory of Harry Scanlan and Dave Grieve August 2014

A rising spring. Too dry for woe in the lime baked valley; it nearly
runs to surface and floods in Mabey's wood at the back of his house,
not country or town, broken bits of old pastoral left behind.

The name remains, deep in memory and history, suits the weekdays
of funerals, everything underground or evaporated to air,
Uncle Harry and poet Dave, their living worlds carried in bulk
and strength and a renegade smile, no corpse ever tells the beauty
of a life, the intricacies of their forest thoughts, the battles,
their woven delights. Harry, flying his Spitfire in clouds, at 20
ready for his first mission, the secret one you don't come back from,
cancelled on the eve by the late blooming death of Hiroshima.
Dave, a sea-dog swaggerer who stored up grief in poetry for famine
-eyed Ethiopians who watched the Navy walk by. 'Don't look,
you cannot help them' were the orders. They belong to Woewater
of the last century, its lost courses, its post war hopes dried up.

We look back, bombardments ended, at the price of the All Clear.
Even that is nibbled away by encroachment on old fields, departing
signals, flow of the underground spring covered by silt, loss, leaves.

Woewater

Belsen, Dachau, those terrible names once innocent. The spring rises
and spills onto shoes of soldiers. The films are grey and white,
bleached almost by the desert of bodies, thousands like pebbles
on a beach ditched by an ever-retreating tide, the living wander
with shut eyes. The burgher-masters and their wives walk two by two
through the camps, the neighbours and farmers invited to witness
a distress so close to their back doors. They walk through avenues
of silence and contempt. The grieving dead are everywhere, acres
of starvation and deluge, so many, and among them the living-dead
with spindles for arms and legs; and eyes like opaque water.
The films are their consecration, they will always be at the gates
of Dis, passing over like ghosts of shadows, barely a flicker within,
as their bodies are laden into pits for safety and bulldozed for safety
under the helm of the earth. The living will be comforted by soldiers.

Women could not be helped, adrift, vacant, young and old, without
measurement of land. 'They were dehumanised. Nothing could reach
them for two weeks – until clothes were sent.' A jumble. Everything
human had been stolen except a tiny kernel, a tiny piece of vanity,
mortal and indestructible, the smallest of flowers in seed. O clothes,
O frivolous clothes, O adornment and unnecessary haberdashery.
O hats and belts and matching accessories, O skirts and shoes
and furbishments of veils and fringes, O pretty jumpers, blouses
and substantial frocks. Yours is the honour the power and the glory.

Holocaust memorial week 2015

The Secret Book of England

for Natasha & Charlie Grigg

I

A yard across in English measure, conjured in a dreamscape,
the book had many pages of pastoral, a land of green dales
and hills in June fullness, trees heavy with leaves, oceans
of trees in billows, hedgerows with late May, cream held
in bud in the chalices of the hawthorn, England under canopy
of long evenings stretching to midsummer. The great book
was blank at first gaze, the pages shone black, shimmering
without power, until tilted to the horizon. We lifted the book
to eye level, as if swimming in calm water, flower meadows
in relief by this angle, lost fields unlocked on this plane, how
can I explain the effort of this undertaking, a mind sleeping
and assembling pages of England, keeping and keeping
each one, addressed to the American family of my son.
The book was not mine except to pass on, a love invisible.

Nothing but the heart's enclosure. What fell to my hand
was the naming of cricket and all its pageantry but the dream
ended before I began, and I knew the book was still open.

II

A ball was flying as birds fly at dusk or dawn for the sake
of flight, and no one moved. The willow like a wand in the aspect
of a spear, a blade, an upright sword aloft like Excalibur,
was his bat swift in the wind, the man and bat the spirit
of the woodland like a poet with words in his head
flying to the corners of his mind onto the air, visible.
The ball was a bird free and obedient, swift as if mastered
by a spirit in the word, in the willow, in the batsman.
The veil dropped for a moment from the world and the crowd
was silent. He took 19 runs from the over in the shiver
of the wind, not a destroyer, a creator. Cricket is ballad
and roundel, saga and battle, ballet and courtship, nuance
and romance of ancient lays as Bell strokes the air like a lyre.

The Catford Constitutional

for Rachel & Julian

Faux dark interiors and old glamour as the Catford Club revives
under treatment of fashionable dereliction upheld by touches of art
and nouvelle degraded décor, copying the romance of the French

chateaux all crumbling plaster and patches on the wall, or even
closer to our hearts, the French Left Bank of moody nonchalance
and dim lit tables where artists and poets ask for Pimms, you can't buy

the atmosphere which comes cheap for those who push through
the doors; Catford High Street, all sleazy pavements and kebab shops,
can't compete with high trends of down-at-heel arty insouciance

where customers are part of the show, dressing up for entrances
and exits, and in the languid deportment there is the thrill
of being exotic from another century when the world was full of cafes

in thrall to surrealism, or decadence, and everyone an existentialist.
The Bohemia which lives and moves on, taking its treasures across
the water. *The Catford Constitutional* has a petition we all sign,

but surely its fate is to close down and disappear like an Eastern
palace in the sky held aloft by genies. Its old graceful lines and
long bar could have flown from the British in India, unrestored

and not pukka, still with oodles of charm as they remember the Raj.
Here, utopian dreams of an impossible future cloud the windows.
The High Street unloved and broken. Catford will somehow triumph.

Notes

Moonlight Sonata
'Moonlight Sonata' was the German codename for the Coventry Blitz. The German verb *Coventrieren* (to Coventrate) was coined by Goebbels to describe the annihilation of a city by aerial bombardment. 'Blessing' is from the old English for bleeding (ie the wounds of Christ).

Shepherd's Hey
The Morris tune of the title was collected in Ilmington, Warwickshire, by Cecil Sharp in 1908.

Clap Bellhead Angel Boyhood
The title of this poem is from Barry McSweeney's *The Book of Demons.*

Dark History
Park Level lead-mine at Killhope on the North Pennines was closed in 1910, but reopened during the First World War.

A Stone for Bill Martin
Bill Martin (1925-2010) was a poet and artist who lived in the North-East. A 'throstle' is a song thrush.

Lines on 'Already Broken'
Linda Saunders' poem 'Already Broken' is published in *The Watchers* (2009).

The German Hotel
The Aguait Hotel, Es Carregador, Mallorca, was taken over by German proprietors. *Vela* is Spanish for sail and candle.

Edgeland
Ovid tells us that the nymphs wept so bitterly for Marsyas their tears formed a river.

Woewater
The 'lost' film of the British liberation of Dachau and Bergen-Belsen, *German Concentration Camps Factual Survey*, produced by Sidney Bernstein, edited by Alfred Hitchcock and scripted by Richard Crossman was thought too terrible to show post war. Excerpts were shown on Channel 4 in *Night Must Fall* 70 years later.

The Secret Book of England
The Bell innings described in this poem was in a T20 game at the Riverside, Durham, 2015.

Acknowledgements

Thanks are due to the editors of the following publications where some of these poems were first published: *The Nightwatchman, Ofi Press Magazine, Tears in the Fence*, the T-Junction international poetry festival anthology 2016; Diane Cockburn et al (eds) *Collecting Stones* (2008), Andy Croft *et al* (eds) *How Things Are Made: Poems for Gordon Hodgeon* (2009), Kevin Cadwallender (ed) *By Grand Central Station We Sat Down and Wept* (2010), Annie Wright *et al* (eds) *NorthBOUND* (2016) and Neil Astley (ed) *Land of the Three Rivers* (2017).

'Notes Towards a Death Bed' was translated into Mallorquin ('Notes Cap a Llit de Mort') by Miquel Llull and published in English and Mallorquin in *Cap Vermell* 2014.

'Springtime of the Nations' was commended in the National Poetry Competition 2011.

My special thanks to poets Linda Saunders, Marilyn Longstaff, Annie Wright, Jo Colley, Cynthia Fuller, Jennifer Grigg, to my son Ben Levitas and daughter Rachel Levitas, and to Vane Women writing collective, for invaluable advice and support.